Disney's Year Book

1988

Disney's
Year Book
1988

GROLIER ENTERPRISES INC.
Danbury, Connecticut

GROLIER ENTERPRISES INC.
Robert B. Clarke   *Publisher*

ISBN: 0-7172-8200-7
ISSN: 0273-1274

Illustration Credits and Acknowledgments

6—© Michael Evans/Sygma; 7—AP/Wide World; 8—Independence
National Historical Park Collection; 9—top, White House Historical
Society; bottom left, Courtesy National Portrait Gallery, London; bottom right, Courtesy Yale University Art Gallery; 10—© Tom Mihalek/
Sygma; 11—© Tom Mihalek/Sygma; 12—Daniel Forster/Duomo; 13—
© Daniel Forster /Duomo; 14—AP/Wide World; 15—© Daniel Forster/Duomo; 28—Children's Television Workshop; 29—Nigel Dickson/
Owl TV; 30—Children's Television Workshop; 31—Compliments Owl
TV; 32—SHOWTIME; 33—Compliments Owl TV; 34—Dot & Sy Barlow; 36—A. Hagood/National Park Service; 37—left, Courtesy Department of Library Services/American Museum of Natural History;
right, Courtesy Department of Library Services/American Museum of
Natural History; 39—Courtesy Denver Museum of Natural History; 52
—© 1986 Arthur Singer Photography; 53—© Ann Purcell; 54—top, ©
Alain Guillou; bottom, © Bob Burch/West Stock; 55—© Carl Purcell;
56—© 1987 The Walt Disney Company; 57-58—© 1937 The Walt Disney Company; 59—© 1987 The Walt Disney Company; 60—Craft by
Jenny Tesar; 74-77—Courtesy Scholastic Photography Awards, conducted by Scholastic Magazines, Inc. and sponsored by Eastman
Kodak Company; 78—© Michael Habicht/Animals, Animals; 79—©
Richard Kolar/Animals, Animals; 80—© Anthony Bannister/Animals,
Animals; 81—© Robert Lee/Photo Researchers, Inc.; 82—© Soames
Summerhays/Photo Researchers, Inc.; 83—© Jerry Cooke/Animals,
Animals.

Contents

Four Sheets of Parchment— Written with a Feather Quill

Schoolchildren examining the Constitution.

Through the summer of 1787, a group of 55 men met in Philadelphia's Independence Hall. Among them were the most important Americans of this time—George Washington, Benjamin Franklin, James Madison, and Alexander Hamilton. The delegates' goal was to create a new form of government for the young country of the United States.

They produced a document that set forth the laws of the country and, for the first time, truly joined the states together into a nation.

Fireworks explode over Independence Hall, where delegates met to write the Constitution.

Sitting above the delegates, George Washington was the presiding officer of the Convention.

The document was, of course, the Constitution of the United States—four sheets of parchment, written with a feather quill.

The delegates to the Constitutional Convention did not have an easy job. There were many fierce and bitter arguments, and the delegates had to compromise on many issues. The result was that few of them agreed with *all* the provisions of the Constitution. George Washington said that he

What the Convention Did

After America won its independence from Great Britain, the nation's government was weak. There was no president. The Congress had little power over the 13 states, each of which pursued its own aims. The Constitution set up a strong central government which unified the country.

James Madison *kept a record of the secret debates in Philadelphia.*

Benjamin Franklin *urged approval of the new Constitution.*

Alexander Hamilton *was in favor of a strong government.*

For 200th anniversary celebration , marchers wore 18th Century costumes (above and right).

didn't expect it to last more than 20 years. But the Constitution survived—and was recognized as an inspired creation.

In 1987, Americans hailed the Constitution's 200th anniversary. There were numerous ceremonies and celebrations. And there was renewed interest in the Constitution itself. Philadelphia, naturally, was the site of some of the most important events. The city staged exhibits, parades and concerts.

One purpose of the bicentennial events was to encourage Americans to learn more about the Constitution. Polls showed that many people did not know some of its basic provisions—for example, only four of every 10 people knew that the first 10 amendments make up the Bill of Rights.

As part of the anniversary celebration, organizations distributed millions of copies of the Constitution. The hope was that more and more Americans would take the time to read and understand our nation's most precious document.

The America's Cup—
Back From Down Under

The countdown to the 1987 America's Cup began with two preliminary competitions.

First, six yachts from the host country of Australia raced against each other for the honor of defending the Cup.

Second, the countries challenging for the Cup raced to see which one would compete against Australia.

The Australian winner was a yacht named *Kookaburra III*. (The kookaburra is a large Australian bird.)

The winner of the international competition was the American yacht *Stars & Stripes*, whose skipper was Dennis Connor. He had been the skipper of *Liberty*, which lost to

Stars & Stripes *leads* Kookaburra III *(left) as they sail 24.3 mile course.* Stars & Stripes' *crew (below) performed flawlessly as the U.S. won.*

Victorious Stars & Stripes *enters the harbor of Fremantle after winning the final race.*

Australia in the 1983 race at Newport, Rhode Island.

In the America's Cup competition, the yacht that won four out of seven races would win the Cup. The races were held off the coast of Fremantle in Western Australia, where the winds are generally strong. *Stars & Stripes* was rated as the faster yacht. It was expected to do better in strong winds, which produce greater speed. *Kookaburra III* was considered to be the more maneuverable yacht. It was expected to do better in lighter breezes because it would be able to turn, or tack, faster.

The contest turned out to be one-sided. In both light and strong winds, Connors outsailed the Australians. *Stars & Stripes* won the first four races and took home the Cup.

THE STORY OF THE AMERICA'S CUP

In 1851, the schooner America *won a yacht race around England's Isle of Wight and took home a silver cup. The New York Yacht Club renamed the trophy the America's Cup and decided to sponsor races with the cup as the prize. The races, too, became known as the America's Cup. From 1870 to 1983, an American yacht won all of the 24 America's Cup races. In 1983, Australia won the cup. In 1987, skipper Dennis Connor (above) sailed the U.S. to victory.*

Big Day For A Small Knight

Once upon a time, there were five knights
in the kingdom of Saint Ives. Sir Bramwell
the Brave was the bravest. Sir Webster the
Wise was the smartest. Sir Quentin the Quick
was the fastest, and Sir Val the Vain was the
most handsome.

The fifth knight was the smallest, and he didn't seem at all special. His name was Sir Percy. The other knights called him Sir Percy the Puny behind his back.

The one thing Sir Percy wanted most was for the King to notice him. He wanted the King to invite him to dinner. He wanted to sit next to the King's beautiful daughter, Princess Penny. He wanted the princess to notice him.

But the King never asked Sir Percy to dinner. He never sat next to the Princess. And the Princess didn't even know who Sir Percy was.

Poor Sir Percy! He had only one friend, and that was a pigeon. It was a very ordinary pigeon, plain gray in color. Its name was Pip.

The other knights thought Sir Percy and his pigeon friend were pretty funny. They laughed and laughed—behind Sir Percy's back.

Sir Percy overheard them. So did Pip. "Don't worry, Pip," said Sir Percy. "Someday they'll notice us. Someday they won't laugh."

Then one day a terrible dragon came to the kingdom! The King called his knights together.

"Do something!"
he commanded.

Sir Quentin the Quick,
Sir Bramwell the Brave,
Sir Webster the Wise
and Sir Val the Vain
all volunteered to
fight the dragon.

Then Sir Percy
spoke up. "Excuse
me, Your Majesty,"
he said to the King.

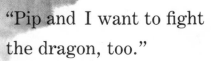

"Pip and I want to fight
the dragon, too."

Well, the other knights
all laughed. After all,
Sir Percy *was* a bit
puny, and the dragon
was a very big dragon.

But the King told

them to stop laughing. "Sir Percy may fight the dragon, too," he said.

So the five knights rode off to the cave where the dragon lived.

"This is where the dragon lives," said Sir Webster, wisely.

"Let's rush in and surprise him!" said Sir Quentin, quickly.

"I'll go in first," said Sir Bramwell, bravely.

"Let me just polish my armor," said Sir Val, vainly.

"I will do what is necessary," said Sir Percy in his small voice.

The other knights were about to laugh at Sir Percy again when they heard a mighty roar.

Sir Bramwell bravely stepped up to the cave and pulled out his sword. But flames

leaped out at him and melted both his sword
and his shield.

Sir Webster tried to think of something
smart to do. "Hurry, Sir Webster!" said Sir
Quentin.

Just then the dragon poked his head out of
the cave and breathed more fire at them.

"Somebody do something," cried Sir Val.
"My armor will get tarnished!"

But the dragon kept breathing fire from his cave. The knights backed away from the heat, toward a deep hole. Then into the hole they tumbled.

They waited for the dragon to attack them, but nothing happened. He roared twice, then ran off toward the town.

"We must warn the King," said Sir Percy. But even Sir Webster the Wise didn't know

how to do that, since they were all trapped in the hole.

Then Sir Percy took out a pen and some paper and wrote a note. He put the note in Pip's beak. "It's up to you, Pip," he said.

The little gray pigeon soared out of the pit. Pip flew straight to the King and dropped the note in his lap.

The King read the note. "A mirror?" he mused. Then he understood. "Come," he said to his guards. "We have much to do."

When the dragon got to the town, he had a big surprise. Instead of seeing houses and shops, he saw a ferocious, fire-breathing dragon! The other dragon was as big as he was! He took one look and ran away, far away from the kingdom of Saint Ives.

The knights didn't get back to Saint Ives until the next day. They were afraid they

might find the town all burned down, but they found a party instead. The guest of honor at the party was Pip, the ordinary gray pigeon! And as soon as the people saw Sir Percy, they cheered!

The other knights couldn't understand it, so the King explained. Sir Percy had sent Pip to him with a message. The note had told the King to put Sir Val's mirror (which was very big) at the edge of town. "When the dragon saw himself, he was so scared that he'll never be back," chuckled the King.

Then the King made a proclamation: "This day belongs to Sir Percy and Pip. Without their help, the dragon would have destroyed us all."

That night the King invited Sir Percy to dinner. The small knight sat right next to the pretty Princess. And now Princess Penny definitely knew who he was—Sir Percy the Proud!

TV FOR KIDS:
Making Learning Fun

Television has finally gotten the message:
Learning can be fun. "Sesame Street" led the
way, and now a new crop of children's shows
is proving that TV for kids can be highly
entertaining and educational, too.

One example is "Owl/TV," the television version of the popular Canadian nature magazine, *Owl*. On this public TV show, intended for kids from seven to 12 years of age, youngsters explore the worlds of animals, science, and the environment in entertaining features.

In *The Mighty Mites*, three children shrink to miniature size (with the help of trick photography.) In their tiny forms, they "get into" some very small places—for example, a fish tank full of guppies.

On "3-2-1 Contact" (left) kids travel around the world to learn about architecture. On "Owl/TV" (below) children explore nature and science.

In *Animals Close Up*, kids go on location to talk with animal experts and observe the animals these experts deal with—for example, a laboratory where bats are studied.

In *You and Your Body*, one of the show's most popular stars, a comic skeleton named Bonapart, helps viewers to understand how the body works.

"Square One" teaches math using amusing skits such as this one starring Shari Belefonte Harper.

Dr. Zed, a brilliant scientist, guides children through scientific experiments on "Owl/TV."

Two other highly successful and entertaining educational shows for children, "Square One" and "3-2-1 Contact," are aimed at a slightly older age group, kids from eight to 12 years of age. Both are seen on public television stations.

"Square One" teaches kids about mathematics through the use of entertaining skits, riddles and animated cartoons.

"3-2-1 Contact" makes science and technology exciting and understandable as young hosts travel around the world in search of scientific information. Each week, the daily

*"Faerie Tale Theatre"' features famous
performers, such as Christopher Reeve
and Bernadette Peters in "Sleeping Beauty."*

episodes are about a different theme, such as
space, electricity or flight.

For a change of pace from science and
nature, children can watch the world's best-

known fairy tales on "Faerie Tale Theatre," which is broadcast on the Showtime cable TV network. Among the two dozen hour-long productions presented so far have been "Hansel and Gretel" and "Cinderella."

The show was conceived by actress Shelley Duvall, and she enlisted the support of television and Hollywood's leading actors, directors and writers. The show's many awards underline the point that children's television can be good—and good for you.

On "Owl/TV," a wise-cracking skeleton teaches children how the human body works.

WHERE DID ALL
THE DINOSAURS GO?

*Some dinosaurs were as small as a sparrow.
Others were huge. The largest known
dinosaur was 60 feet high and weighed
about 160,000 pounds.*

For 160 million years, there were dinosaurs on the Earth. Then, mysteriously, 65 million years ago, all the dinosaurs died out.

Why did dinosaurs disappear? Scientists called paleontologists try to find the answer to this question. Paleontologists study plants and animals that lived long ago. To find out about dinosaurs, they study the fossil remains of these animals.

A fossil may be part of a dinosaur, such as a tooth or bone that has been preserved in a rock. Over many thousands of years, the tooth or bone may itself have turned into rock but kept its original shape. A fossil may also be just an outline or impression in a rock, such as a footprint.

The scientists who study dinosaurs are like detectives. The fossil clues they collect help them to solve the mystery of what dinosaurs were like, how they lived and why they died out.

WERE DINOSAURS LIKE LIZARDS?

The name "dinosaur" comes from the Greek words meaning "terrible lizard." Scientists

Scientists chip away rock from a dinosaur fossil so that they can examine bones more carefully.

long believed that, since dinosaurs looked like lizards, they were cold-blooded, as lizards are.

The body temperature of a cold-blooded animal like a lizard becomes warmer or colder as the temperature of the air becomes warmer or colder. In contrast, warm-blooded animals like birds and human beings have a body temperature that stays the same, no matter how cold or warm the air becomes.

Cold-blooded animals generally are sluggish and slow moving. Cold-blooded dinosaurs would also be sluggish and move slowly. But recent studies of dinosaur fossils show that many dinosaurs were not slow-moving at all. Some could run as fast as 30 miles per hour.

The new fossil studies also show that at least some dinosaurs behaved like warm-blooded animals in other ways, too. Some dinosaurs stood on their hind legs instead of

A fossil of a dinosaur's skin (below) shows its scaly texture. By measuring fossil foot-prints (right), scientists can estimate a dinosaur's size.

Diplodocus was a plant-eating dinosaur. One of the largest known dinosaurs, it grew to be 85 feet long and weighed about 30,000 pounds.

hugging the ground as lizards do. And some dinosaurs cared for their young, as birds do.

From this evidence, scientists have concluded that at least some dinosaurs were warm-blooded. If they were warm-blooded, these dinosaurs would not have died out simply because the temperature of the Earth became much colder. Or because they could not compete with faster-moving mammals.

WHAT HAPPENED TO DINOSAURS?

Some scientists now believe that dinosaurs died out after a large meteorite—a solid body from space—crashed into the Earth. This crash created a cloud of dust that blocked sunlight from reaching the Earth. Without

sunlight, many plants died out, and the animals that ate them died, too.

This theory has not been proved. Other scientists continue to believe that dinosaurs died out over a long period of time as conditions on Earth changed in various ways. Dinosaurs were not able to adapt to these changes.

But scientists are still trying to discover exactly how and why these changes took place—and so the mystery of why dinosaurs disappeared still remains.

The Wind Lion

Bambi and Thumper were watching all the forest animals get ready for winter.

Squirrels were busy gathering acorns. Ground hogs were lining their dens with nice, soft grass. Bears were looking for cozy caves. Big flocks of geese were flying overhead, going south where the weather would be warmer.

"Look!" said Bambi. "There's one goose that's flying away from the rest!"

"He's coming down here!" cried Thumper.

"Let's go see him!"

They arrived just in time to see a 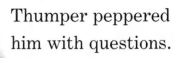 big Canada goose land on the pond. The bird swam over to the bank and struggled out of the water, dragging its wings.

"Are you all right?" asked Thumper. "Did you hurt your wing? Are you going to stay?"

"Hooold on, little rabbit," said the goose in a tired voice. "I'll answer you after I have a nap." And the goose tucked his head under his wing and was soon asleep.

When the goose finally opened his eyes,

Thumper peppered him with questions. Patiently, the goose answered. He told how he had been leading the way for the flock during a storm. When the storm was over, he was so tired that he hadn't been able to continue south with the rest of the flock. He had decided to rest on the pond until he was strong enough to continue his journey.

Both Thumper and Bambi thought the goose was very brave. They were afraid of storms.

In the days that followed, the goose told Bambi and Thumper stories about flying, and Canada, and the big lakes.

But the story they   liked
best was the one about the
wind lion. They made him
tell that one over and over.
The goose would describe
the lion, and Bambi and
Thumper would shiver.
"It has the head, feet

and tail of a lion,
the body of an eagle,
and large, powerful
wings. They sound
like this." And the
goose would flap his
own large, powerful
wings, so the air
made a scary,
whooshing sound.

"And when the wind lion
gets mad," continued the goose,
"it roars like thunder."

"How do you make a wind lion mad?" asked
Thumper in a small voice.

"By asking too many questions," chuckled
the goose. Then he saw the scared look on
Thumper's face.

"There's a way to get rid of a wind lion

when you've made it angry," said the goose. "You look straight into its face and . . ." He paused for effect.

"And what?" begged Thumper.

"Tell it to go away," said the goose with a playful wink. "Now, you youngsters better go home," he added, ruffling his feathers. "It sounds like there's a storm coming up."

As Bambi and Thumper made their way home, the trees began to take on strange

45

shapes in the darkening forest. The wind blew harder, making a spooky whistling sound. Suddenly Bambi and Thumper heard a rumble of thunder.

"What if it's the wind lion?" asked Thumper.

"Better stop asking questions," answered Bambi.

When rain began
to fall, Bambi and
Thumper ducked into a
thicket. They knew it
wasn't safe to stay out in a
storm. As they sheltered there, the rain poured
down harder and harder, and thunder rumbled.
Thumper couldn't get the wind lion out of his
mind.

Then, just as the rain stopped, they heard
the sound of powerful, beating wings.

Whoosh, whoosh, whoosh!

"It's the wind lion!" cried Thumper.

They heard the sound again, this time
closer. Thumper was trembling with fear.
Bambi was afraid, too, but he gathered all his
courage and jumped out into the open. Above
him he heard the sound of beating wings. He
looked up and yelled with all his might: "Go
away, wind lion!"

"Bambi, is that you?" called the familiar voice of the goose. The great bird landed in front of him.

"I was worried you might not get home safely," explained the goose, "so I came to look for you."

Thumper stuck his nose out of the thicket. "We were hiding from the wind lion," he said. "You must have scared him away."

The goose laughed. "What you thought was the wind lion was only the sound of my wings," he said.

"You mean there was no wind lion?" said Bambi.

"No, son," the goose replied. "That was just a story." And he took Bambi and Thumper home to their mothers.

The next morning, when Bambi and Thumper went down to the pond, they couldn't find the goose.

"He didn't even say goodbye," said Thumper.

"He shouldn't have left without saying goodbye," Bambi complained to his mother later.

"He knew you were safe," she said. "He had to leave, you know. He must fly south before it gets too cold.

"And, you know, you'll always remember him," his mother added. "Every time you get scared, just remember the goose and his story of the wind lion. He taught you that if you face your fears, you often find that there was nothing to fear, after all."

BIG BALLOONS

Hot-air balloons are bigger than they used to be. And they don't always look like balloons used to look. These days, a balloon may look like an elephant or a house, a tiger or a floating version of Uncle Sam.

Bright-colored balloons are launched at a festival in Somers, N.Y. (above). Uncle Sam smiles down from high in the sky (right).

The hot air in a balloon is lighter than the surrounding air and this makes the balloon rise. Until recently, the air in a hot-air balloon was heated while the balloon was on the ground. Once the balloon took off, the air cooled and the balloon came down.

Unusual balloons such as the elephant (above) and the French mansion (below) are flown on special occasions or used for advertising. The tiger (right) advertises a breakfast cereal.

Today's balloons use a small propane heater to keep the air hot as they fly. That means they can stay up longer. Modern balloons are made of tough synthetic fabrics. These fabrics made it possible to make balloons in unusual shapes.

Hot air ballooning is becoming a highly popular sport—and part of the fun is to fly the biggest, most unusual balloon in the sky.

50 Candles
for a Classic

Sneezy sneezed and Grumpy grumped and Dopey did a happy little dance.

All the dwarfs, and Snow White too, celebrated their fiftieth birthday in 1987. In honor of the occasion, Walt Disney Studios made 1987 the Year of Snow White, and fans in more than 60 countries had a chance to see Snow White again and to laugh and cry at the magic of this marvelous movie.

Snow White dances with the dwarfs: Sleepy, Happy, Dopey, Sneezy, Grumpy, Doc, Bashful.

Snow White was first shown in 1937. It was the first full-length animated cartoon, and many people thought it would be a flop. But *Snow White* became one of the most popular films of all time, and is now regarded as one of Hollywood's great classics.

The story of Snow White comes from a fairy tale by the Grimm brothers. But of course, it was what Walt Disney did with the story that created a film full of romance, humor and excitement.

Snow White was the first cartoon character to seem totally human. And the seven dwarfs are inspired creations—each one funny and lovable in a different way.

To celebrate the Year of Snow White, there were special parades at Disneyland in California and Walt Disney World in Florida. Performers dressed as Snow White and the seven dwarfs made special appearances all over America.

In Hollywood, a brass star with Snow White's name on it was put into the sidewalk, next to all the other stars that honor Hollywood's most famous film actors and actresses.

Audiences love Dopey, the sweet, silent dwarf (above left).

New fans greeted Snow White and her handsome Prince when they appeared in parades.

How To Turn 2,533 Beans Into a Duck

Don't try to count the beans in the duck.
You'll get tired of counting. Make your own
duck instead.

What should you do with your duck after
you make it? Hang it on your wall. Then
invite your friends over. Let *them* count the
number of beans.

What You'll Need

Dried beans in different colors. *Look in the supermarket (or your kitchen cupboard) for red kidney beans, brown lentils, green and yellow split peas, speckled pinto beans, and any other colored beans.*

A piece of wood.   Rope.

A pencil.   White glue.

A picture of a duck.

What to Do

1. Sketch or trace the picture of the duck on the wood.

2. Decide which beans you want to use for the duck and its wings and which for the background.

3. Put some glue on a small area of the board. Then put the beans on the glued section. (Be sure you don't cover your tracing!)

4. When you've put all the beans on the board, make a frame using the rope and some dark beans. Glue the beans and the rope to the board.

BAD LUCK FOR LUCKY

Dirt was flying everywhere. Lucky Puppy was digging a deep hole.

"Lucky! It's time for our snack," called his brothers, Patch and Rolly.

Lucky pulled his head out of the hole. Something dangled from his mouth. He dropped it at Patch's feet.

"There!" he said proudly. "What do you think of that?"

"What is it?" said Patch.

"I don't know, but it's real old."

Rolly looked at the object closely. "It's round, and it's got writing on it," he noticed. "Maybe it's an ancient necklace. Maybe the writing is an evil spell.

"Remember that movie we saw on television, *The Egyptian Ring?* The king who found that ring had awful luck."

"Aw, that was just a movie," said Lucky with a shrug. He put the object under a bush and joined his brothers in the kitchen.

But Nanny frowned at him. "You naughty puppy," she scolded. "You've been digging again."

So while everyone else ate biscuits and milk, Lucky got a bath.

"Don't wiggle," ordered Nanny, rubbing him hard with a towel. But Lucky couldn't help wiggling. His brothers and sisters were in the living room cheering for his television hero, Thunderbolt the Wonder Dog.

Nanny put Lucky down on the floor, and he

took off like a shot. He didn't want to miss his favorite show. He skidded around the corner into the living room. He was going so fast that he ran into the table leg with a dull thud. Then there was a loud crash.

Nanny came running. She found Lucky sitting among the pieces of a broken flower vase.

"Lucky!" she cried. "You know better than to run in the house!" And Nanny carried him to the kitchen and put him in a corner.

Lucky moped in the kitchen while his brothers and sisters watched the Thunderbolt show. When it was over, Patch and Rolly joined him.

"I told you that thing you found was bad luck," said Rolly. "Look at the trouble you've been in today."

"What are you going to do?" asked Patch.

"I'm going to bury it again—somewhere else," Lucky said. "Then maybe the bad luck will leave me."

"We can bury it in the park tonight," suggested Rolly. "That should be far enough away."

That night the three pups slipped quietly out the back door. They took turns digging a hole under the fence.

Lucky was the first to squeeze through, holding the necklace between his teeth. Patch followed, calling back to Rolly, "Hurry! It's getting late."

"I can't get through," cried Rolly. His chubby body wouldn't fit through the hole they had made.

"Then you'll have to stay here," said Patch.

Rolly pulled his head back into the yard and sat down. Sadly he watched Patch and

Lucky disappear down the dark street.

By the time the two pups reached the park, it was really dark, and all the trees made dark, spooky shapes. "The park sure looks different at night," said Patch. They hurried along.

Soon Lucky found a place to bury his find. He dug a hole and dropped the necklace into it. Then Patch growled. "I hear footsteps."

"I hear them, too," Lucky whispered.

"They're coming through the bushes."

Both pups stared at the bushes. But all they could see were black branches that made strange shapes. The noises came closer.

"I'm afraid," whispered Patch. His voice trembled.

Lucky was afraid, too, but he barked, "Who's there?"

The footsteps began running. Branches snapped. The creature was coming toward them. It sounded large and horrible.

"It's that bad luck you dug up," groaned Patch. The bushes rattled. Suddenly a white shadow leaped out.

"Boy, am I glad to see you guys!" panted Rolly. "I finally got through the fence, but then I got lost in the park. If you hadn't barked, Lucky, I would never have found you." Then Rolly noticed how quiet his brothers were. "What's the matter?" he asked. "I didn't scare you, did I?"

"Never mind," said Lucky, and he pushed dirt over the necklace and buried it. "Come on! Let's get out of here!" The three pups ran for home.

The next day Roger and Anita took Pongo and Perdita for a walk in the park. The puppies went, too, all except Lucky, Patch, and Rolly who were too sleepy to go.

Lucky's feet were kicking out. He was
having a bad dream about an unlucky
Egyptian necklace. Then he woke up.

Roger had rushed in. "Nanny!" he called
out. "Look what Pongo found in the park!"

Lucky was horrified. Roger was holding up
the bad-luck necklace he had buried last
night!

"What on earth is that?" Nanny asked.

"It's a medal for bravery," answered
Roger. "It belonged to my father. I thought
Pongo had buried it in the backyard when he
was a pup."

Roger reached down and gave Pongo a pat
on the head. "I don't know what it was doing
in the park," he said, "but at least I have
found it again. This must be my lucky day."

"Mine, too," thought Lucky. And he
breathed a sigh of relief.

PHOTO MAGIC

The camera is a magic machine that lets the photographer record an image on film. But it is the photographer who performs the real magic by selecting something to shoot that is unusual, interesting or just plain beautiful. For proof of that, just look at the prize-winning photographs on these pages.

For Esme *(left) by Elizabeth Fox, 17, Winter Garden, Florida.* Spiral into Web of Light *(right) by Mike Merriman, 16, Columbus, Ohio.* Crayons and Spruttle *(below) by Robbie Parker, 15, Miami, Florida.*

Reflection by Hand *(left) by Jimmie Hirabayashi, 17, Palos Verdes, California.* Untitled *(above) by Bryan Horne, 17, Burbank, California.*

The photographs on these pages were among the winners in the 1987 Scholastic/Kodak Photo Award Program. This program is open to students in junior and senior high schools in the United States and Canada. The winners receive scholarships and other awards.

When Is a Nose More Than a Nose?

Animal noses come in hundreds of sizes and shapes, from a pig's snout to an elephant's hose-like trunk. Animals use their noses for many things besides smelling—as hands and tools and weapons, to greet friends, warn enemies and spank their children.

The star-nosed mole uses its strange nose to find food. It eats half its weight every day.

THAT'S A NOSE?

The star-nosed mole has one of the strangest-looking noses of all animals. The star-nosed mole is almost blind. It uses the 22 fleshy feelers around its nostrils to find its way through underground tunnels and to locate the worms and insects it eats.

HAVE TRUNK WITH TALENT

An elephant's trunk, or nose, can grow to six feet in length, and no animal's nose is more talented. With the nostrils at the tip of its nose, an elephant can smell water that's three miles away.

Many animals, including dogs, have a better sense of smell than humans do. The bloodhound can smell a person from one-half a mile away.

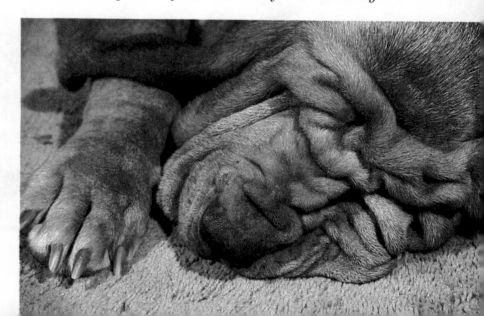

An elephant's trunk is very strong. It has more than 40,000 muscles and it's powerful enough to lift 2,000 pounds of logs. Yet the end of the trunk is delicate enough to grab a single peanut!

Elephants use their trunks for many purposes. They "talk" by making noises

Friendly elephants often twist their trunks together to greet each other when they meet.

A hummingbird uses its slim beak and long tongue to get the nectar out of flowers.

through their trunks. Mother elephants show affection by stroking their babies with their trunks. And they spank a child by giving it a hard whack.

BEAKS ARE NOSES, TOO

A bird's nose is where its mouth is. Its beak, or bill, is really a combination of nostrils and lips. For a bird, a beak serves as both a hand and a tool. Birds use their beaks to find, catch, kill and eat their food.

The spoonbill's large beak is shaped like a spoon, which it uses to dig up frogs and fish from a muddy river bank.

The shark's keen nose can smell one ounce of fish blood in one million ounces of sea water.

The spoonbill announces its return to its nest by opening and closing its beak quickly to make a loud, clapping noise.

STOP GROWING, PLEASE!

The prize for the most unusual nose goes to the proboscis monkey, an animal that lives in Borneo.

The proboscis monkey is born with a cute, turned-up nose—but the nose keeps growing. When the monkey is fully grown, its nose is often so long it hangs down over its mouth, and the monkey has to push it aside to eat.

When a male honks to call its mate, its long nose fills with sound and acts like an echo chamber. The nose makes the sound much louder, so it can be heard over a greater distance.

The nose of a proboscis monkey starts small, but it gets bigger and bigger as the animal grows.

DONALD'S DAY OFF

Daisy Duck was having a lemonade one
afternoon when Donald stopped by. He
looked tired.

Daisy poured him a lemonade. "What's the
matter, Donald?" she asked.

"I worked so hard today," said Donald. "I
wish I could be like you and stay home."

"Just because I stay home doesn't mean I
don't work," Daisy pointed out.

"Ha! I could do your housework with one
hand tied behind my back," boasted Donald.
"One day at *my* job would make you tired,
too."

"We'll see about that, Donald," said Daisy.
"Tomorrow we'll switch places."

"It's a deal," Donald agreed, grinning.

The next morning, Donald arrived with a
stack of comic books, all ready for a day of
housework. Daisy was dressed up, all ready
for a day of office work. She left Donald a list
of the things that had to be done.

At first, Donald's day went fine. He
watered the yard, took out the trash and
washed the dishes. Then he made himself a
snack and lay down to read his comic books
for a few minutes.

When Donald woke up, it was late. But he
wasn't worried. He
only had washing the
clothes and vacuuming
the living room left.

"But that'll be easy. I can even surprise
Daisy by cooking dinner," he thought.

Donald started to prepare dinner when he
heard the dog and cat at the back door. He
had forgotten to feed them.

Daisy had told him to feed the dog and cat

outside. But Donald let them into the kitchen
and fed them. Then he went back to his
cooking.

Donald had decided to make a fancy
dessert first. He got out all the ingredients

and began to mix and stir. The dog wagged
his tail, and the cat began to purr. They liked
the eggs and milk and sugar that Donald was
pouring into the mixing bowl.

Just then the telephone rang. Donald went
to answer it and took a message for Daisy.
"While I'm here in the living room," he said
to himself, "I might as well vacuum the rug.
But first, I'll start the laundry."

Donald forgot all about his fancy dessert.

In the laundry room, Donald found some
piles of clothes. It would take a long time to
wash each pile separately, so he decided to
put them all in the washer at once.

"I'll use a cup of soap for each load of clothes," he figured, proud of getting so much work done so easily.

When he turned on the washer, it groaned, but Donald paid no attention.

Next, Donald went back to the living room and started the vacuum cleaner. It was a very big one, and Donald had to push it very

hard. Soon he was tired. Then he remembered
his dessert.

"Oh, my goodness!" he exclaimed. "I must
put my dessert in the oven now, or it'll never
be ready by the time Daisy gets home." And
he rushed off to the kitchen, leaving the
vacuum running in the middle of the rug.

But what had happened to the dessert?
There was nothing in the bowl—but the cat
and dog were licking their whiskers.

Donald was mad. He chased the animals outside and started all over again. Again he mixed and stirred, then poured the dessert into a pan and put it in the oven. It was supposed to cook for an hour, at medium temperature. But Daisy would be home sooner than that! Donald decided to cook the dessert twice as fast, at twice the temperature.

It sounded like a good idea. Just then, Donald heard funny noises coming from the living room. He ran in and

saw the rug disappearing into the vacuum cleaner!

"Wak!" cried Donald, and he pulled and pulled. The rug came loose so suddenly that

Donald sat right down on the floor.

Then Donald realized that he was getting wet! "Wak!" he cried again. The washing machine had run over, and soapy water was running all over the floor.

Donald ran into the laundry room and began mopping. Then he smelled something

burning. He ran into the kitchen to find black
smoke seeping out of the oven.

Coughing and gasping, Donald grabbed a
potholder and threw the blackened dessert
into the sink.

Just then, Daisy came home. "Donald, how
was your day?" she called as she came in the
door. Then she gasped. Black smoke filled the
house. Wet footprints ran across the floor.
The rug was tangled in a heap. And poor
Donald was sitting in the middle of the mess
with a dazed expression on his face.

"Oh, Daisy, I'm so sorry!" he gulped. "I
thought it would be easy to do your
housework, but it wasn't."

Donald looked so pitiful that Daisy couldn't
be mad. But she had to teach him a lesson.

"Well, Donald," she said, "Here I am, home after a hard day at the office. What did you make for dinner?"

Donald pointed sadly to the mess in the sink.

"We can't eat that," she said. "We'd better go get a pizza."

"Really?" said Donald, not quite so sadly. "Gee, thanks. I love pizza."

"Good," said Daisy, "because you're treating."

"I guess that's only right," said Donald sheepishly. "I'll even buy us a fancy dessert."